Now Go

Published by 404 Ink Limited
www.404Ink.com
@404Ink

Editing & proofreading: Heather McDaid
Typesetting: Laura Jones
Cover design: Luke Bird
Co-founders and publishers of 404 Ink:
Heather McDaid & Laura Jones

Print ISBN: 978-1-912489-58-9
Ebook ISBN: 978-1-912489-59-6

Printed and bound in Great Britain by Clays Ltd, Elcograf S.p.A.

Now Go

On Grief and Studio Ghibli

Karl Thomas Smith

Inklings

Contents

Spoiler Notes

Now Go touches on many of the films of Studio Ghibli in various levels of detail, and spoilers large and small include:

Grave of the Fireflies
Kiki's Delivery Service
My Neighbor Totoro
Nausicaä of the Valley of the Wind
Ponyo on the Cliff by the Sea
Princes Mononoke
Spirited Away

Introduction
A winking light in the darkness

What do you think of when you hear "Studio Ghibli"?

Elegant, exquisitely translucent, watercolour skies? Sunsets that effortlessly turn from the lightest pastel hues to the most striking halogen glows as they effervesce? The pang of childhood nostalgia and a beguiling sense of wonderment at the beauty of our natural world? Perhaps a style of cloud so unique and so recognisable that it rivals even the best that the real world has to offer – or even a vision of Totoro himself; the culturally ubiquitous gentle giant which has become Ghibli's honorary mascot.

All of these are good answers. Right answers, even. But they are all just a small part of the picture. When I hear "Studio Ghibli", I think of all these things. But there is also something else: not so much a thought as a feeling. Something not rendered in those frames, not contained in those forms and colours, but illuminated by them. You see, I did not grow up with the films of Studio Ghibli. Not in the traditional sense, at least. But I wish that I had.

*

I was twelve when the English-language dub of *Spirited Away* was first released, winning the Academy Award for Best Animated Feature. A short time later, my grand-father – very much a presence in my life until that moment – died from a maelstrom of complications relating to cancer which are so obscure to me, even now, that I could not possibly tell you which of them finally ended his life.

In that film, Chihiro, the pre-teen hero of the piece, is taken from a world she knows and from the people who love her – dragged headfirst and put to work in a bustling bathhouse at the centre of a strange and (under-standably) overwhelming spirit dimension. Her parents transformed into pigs and threatened with the kind of death that unfortunately tends to befall so many of the pigs of this world, she is forced – and there's just no other way to say this – to really *get her shit together*. To put her childhood and her loss on hold, for just as long as it takes, and to *just get through it*. All of which feels like advice I could've definitely used.

By the time I'd learned to appreciate the finer points of the story – come to see it as an allegory for moving through a world in which the people that you love will, inevitably, one way or another, leave you to fend for yourself in a landscape that suddenly seems strange and frightening – I was already some way into the next decade of my life. A time during which, having already given up drinking once, I had very much given up the giving up and started back on it (and other things) again.

I was once more, or perhaps even still, looking for comfort and understanding from a source outside of myself: to paraphrase *Donnie Darko*, another film of my youth, I was a young man looking for *something* in all the wrong places. And so, while I didn't come of age with Ghibli films, I did – eventually, some time later – become myself in their shadow and their glow. For that I will always be grateful.

*

For me, as a kid, Studio Ghibli had been hiding in plain sight. I had seen the DVDs of *Princess Mononoke* on shelves at HMV, the plush toys of popular characters like Totoro in shop windows, and even the companion manga books collected in their multiple parts on dedicated bookstore spinners. All the pieces were there, but something just hadn't quite clicked for me yet. There was no feeling that this should become something important to me – fewer still that it would be.

For plenty of others, I know now that this was already the case. Not just in Japan, where the studio was and continues to be based – or even in the wider East Asian market, by virtue of proximity – but all over the world. What I had been seeing was just the evidence: the result of what, back then, would have already been twenty-five years of work at the very top of the animation game under the Ghibli name, and decades of groundwork before that even began. The combined product of centuries-worth of talent, pooled in perfect harmony.

*

Formed in 1985, Studio Ghibli was – and, at least in spirit, to this day very much still is – the project of its lead director, Hayao Miyazaki, the producer and former company president Toshio Suzuki, and a second acclaimed directing talent in the now sadly-departed Isao Takahata. Yet, as its enigmatic figurehead, and with the commercial success of films like *Spirited Away* and *Howl's Moving Castle*, Miyazaki's name is the one which has become a byword for Ghibli itself. While it is certainly true that he is responsible for so many of its most acclaimed pictures,

Studio Ghibli's output would look very different without the input of its three founding fathers.

Without Takahata, there would be no *Grave of the Fireflies*, a unique and rending tale of familial love and death in wartime rural Japan (and one of those films guaranteed to truly ruin your day and probably the rest of your week), no *Only Yesterday*; a near first-of-its-kind as a realistic animated drama geared toward adults, and no *Tale of Princess Kaguya* – a masterwork of animation which, by all rights, ought to have reinvented the medium altogether, going not so much "back to basics" but back to the impressionistic roots of Japanese visual storytelling. And without Suzuki, whose creative vision brought them together under one roof, there would be no Ghibli filmography at all.

Miyazaki may well be the brightest and most visible star, but his light is far from the only one in the inky Studio Ghibli sky. Ghibli is not just the output of one man – it is more. Much more, even, than the work of those three men combined and the talents of those artists working under their direction.

There's no need here to give you a potted history of Ghibli. Or, at least, I have no desire to do so beyond what you've now already read. After all, you've got access to Wikipedia and its innumerable sources. Instead, this is a book about meaning; about searching for something – fumbling for anything like an "answer" to a not-quite-certain question, in what can often seem like total darkness, and, hopefully, eventually, about finding it somewhere unexpected. In Studio Ghibli.

*

Combining animism, magical realism, and something more like a sense of "near-reality" in its films, Ghibli's unparalleled animated repertoire is a uniquely crystalised vision of the world: a shared dialogue between creators and viewers – between art and reality. Its universe is not so far from our own: there are human beings with recognisably human traits, there's food and drink rendered with famously saliva-inducing aplomb, weather of all the usual and less usual kinds, and all those things we take for granted as being everyday occurrences. But there is also a depth; a deeper magic to that minutiae – elemental spirits and animal gods – ancient beings, acting seen and unseen, as the engine behind it all. Asking us not so much to question what we know but to consider the possibility that there might just be *more*.

In short, it is a gift. A way of seeing, and an enchanted instrument for interpretation. But that does not make Ghibli films, Ghibli characters, or even those unmistakable Ghibli landscapes, a blank slate for the unconscious: these are not voids for projection, but something more like complex, individual realities to be inhabited and intricate narratives through which to move. They are experiences – created not just to be watched, but to be lived.

Like life in general, they are about both the inevitable end-point and the journey.

*

Chosen by Miyazaki, in what might well be called "uncharacteristically romantic" fashion, "Ghibli" is borrowed from the Italian word for a particular kind of hot desert breeze, named with the idea in mind that the studio would – as he put it – 'blow a new wind through the anime industry.' (Although there is also a much more typical video of Miyazaki, simultaneously crochety and good-humoured, laughing with an implied sense of scorn about the fact that "Ghibli" is just a word that he stole from the side of a plane.)

Beyond those auspicious and ambitious roots – or, despite his own dismissiveness of the meaning – Ghibli has proved to be a more appropriate moniker than even Miyazaki could have hoped. It is evocative of the unique feeling that the studio's films stir in those who hold them close – and a constant reminder of why that embrace remains so warm.

In a sense, these films are voices of the past – carried on the air, whispered into our present-day ears: fantasy worlds that do not ask us to forget the one in which we live, but instead remind us to look beyond it. Not to ignore the subjects of sadness and grief and mourning, but to embrace them and – if possible – to find a sense of joy in that embrace, difficult as it may be. Most of us will live, but all of us will die. People. Things. Innocence. Youth. Eventually, even life as we know it.

Death – if nothing else – is certain. And, to that end, the Ghibli filmography is vivid and immersive proof that this outlook on life is not a cold or dispassionate one; not a mark of indifference to the act of being. On the contrary, its magic – both literal and artistic – is testament to the importance of what it is to remember the fact of mortality in all its forms and to own it, rather than allowing it to take ownership over us.

Miyazaki once said that 'life is a winking light in the darkness.' While all evidence suggests that the man himself would likely never suggest something quite so grandiose, Studio Ghibli is also that light for many. These are films which, in their empathy, their honesty, and their artistry, reveal more life and about death than that which they obscure with any sense of fantasy.

I say this not as an impartial observer, but as someone who has found the lens of Studio Ghibli to provide not an escape but a clearer view of this world. Not always the one I have wanted to see, of course, but one that is most necessary.

In 2017, I moved to London and lived alone for the first time. I found myself not only coming home to an empty flat at the end of every day – or every night, or morning, as was so often the case back then – but also to another kind of emptiness. Caught in less of a classic "downward spiral" than in something much less dynamic, everything at the time seemed endlessly neutral and entirely ineffectual. Nothing stuck. I became complacent with life in the more abstract sense, and also in the much more tangible fashion – leaning into a complete disregard for my own wellbeing in the form of a narcotic effort undertaken not to so much to take the edge off, but to make it either make sharp enough to hurt. Or, failing that, to just sleep through the murk of it all.

It is a deep, dark hole that I cannot say I dug my own way out of. At least, not entirely. But there are two things in life that are sure to grab you by the ever-rounding hunch of your shoulders and shake you hard, until the stupid falls out and you are forced to look at it there, all over the floor of your life.

Those things, of course, are love and death. Finding the former at the same time as the latter decides to seek you out and do its thing is the most sobering kind of one-two punch. If you're wondering how all of this lines up with writing about an anime-producing movie studio, the answer is that these are the twin pillars on which that filmography sits: all of the grief and all of the good – the constant conversation between living and dying; the living and the dead – are what flesh out the worlds that Studio Ghibli creates, giving meaning to narratives that might otherwise seem beautiful but banal. In that regard, our own world is really not so different.

All of this came together for me not when I needed it the most – which would be neat, tidy, and very convenient for the purposes of this book – but when I needed it *still*. You cannot, as it turns out, outrun grief or loss. A decade later, even when you don't feel it breathing down your neck, it is there – in the shadows.

You have to find a way to live with it – to beckon it closer, even when that feels counterintuitive. Like the films of Studio Ghibli, the warmth of its embrace may be a pleasant surprise.

So, what do I think of when I think of Studio Ghibli?

Yes, I think of clouds – of hand-drawn landscapes and of sunsets bright enough to make me blink, even through the screen. But I also think of my Grandfather. I think of my Grandmother, who died in early 2018. I think of the love of my life, who I found then and who was there through all of that. I think of a world that is imbued with a sense of more – even when that comes, in part, from what is taken.

Chapter 1
Grief has No-Face

Let me pick up again by following a tried and tested format – well, tested once at least. Another question. A more complicated one, perhaps.

What do you think of when you hear the word "grief"?

Again, there are no wrong answers here. More than anything in this world, grief means different things to different people, even more so than love – although, inevitably, the two are inseparable. Grief takes different shapes, wears different masks depending on its focus. It is difficult to quantify because there is no concrete form – no beginning and no end, no ceiling or floor. It is not a space which, in the throes of loss, you are pushed into inhabiting – a silent, air-tight vacuum from which there is no apparent means of escape. Instead, it is a space that climbs inside of you – a shadow, of sorts, which in your darkest and lowest of moments needs only to find the smallest of openings to slip through; a tiny, shaded corner in which to take root and to grow. Alone, it is a nothingness. To survive and to thrive, it needs a host.

In terms of cinema at least, I can think of no better and clearer example – no more lucid or accessible articulation – than those painted for us by the films of Studio Ghibli: *Grave of the Fireflies*, Isao Takahata's gruelling tale of two siblings in wartime Japan; *Princess Mononoke*, Miyazaki's sprawling story of animal gods, human frailty, and a mask-wearing heroine who links the two; *Spirited Away*, about a young girl who is put to work in a spirit-realm bath house when her parents are turned to pigs; *My Neighbor Totoro*, where two sisters find comfort in the form of a sleepy forest troll – even *Ponyo on the Cliff by the Sea*, about a curious fish who becomes a ham-loving human being and creates a bridge between worlds, which falls more than almost any other Ghibli release into the realm of children's animation. All of these films, some more obviously than others, are centred on grief, on a potent, rupturous loss of some kind.

What is special, then, about the kind of grief which rears its head so frequently in the Ghibli filmography is that, rather than the singular, it is a question of plurality. Not a "kind of grief" at all, but rather a collective of griefs – whatever the group noun for that may be. (A murder seems too obvious and too violent.) Not confined to "death" in the traditional sense, but encompassing it as one of many archetypal feelings of loss.

Among these, there are griefs on different scales – not a measure put in place to say that one type is more important than any other. It is not a question of hierarchy, but rather a sense that there are griefs of varying scope existing alongside one another. The most obvious example of which is the distinction between death, in the familiar and often familial sense, as in the death of a loved one, and death on a cataclysmic measure: personal grief, let's say – the kind of grief which shatters the fabric of your own world and then proceeds to hold the sharpest pieces of its remains against your most tender parts – and something like environmental grief; the kind of pain and loss and mourning which is shared collectively although distributed unfairly. A uniquely contemporary trauma, felt on a global and historical scale, as the very landscape on which those smaller and more intimate losses are played out is itself destroyed and sentenced to death.

Both of these are losses, both weigh heavy, and both are longstanding preoccupations of Hayao Miyazaki and Isao Takahata alike.

Neither has been particularly public over the years – wide-ranging interviews are scarce, even more so in English or in translation – and pinpointing the root cause of these fixations from a third-party perspective would be a whole lot of conjecture punctuated by the odd educated guess. That being said, that Miyazaki's mother suffered from spinal tuberculosis and was hospitalised intensely for several years of his childhood – or the fact, even, that the director himself was once given a prognosis forecasting a lifespan not much more than twenty years – seem like they fall distinctly into the latter category. As does the fact that both Miyazaki and Takahata grew up in the shadow of the Second World War (born in 1941 and 1935 respectively) – old enough, even, to remember Hiroshima and Nagasaki's unconscionable nuclear horror; the death and destruction on a scale previously unimaginable even in the worst of nightmares.

Grief on a national, societal, and cultural level – grief that worked its way not just into the metaphorical hearts of the Japanese people, but also into the physical DNA of so many innocent men, women and children – is a shared part of their own personal history. One which calling "formative" in respect to their attitudes on ecological and personal disaster, to grief of all kinds on all scales, feels like something of an understatement.

It's perhaps unsurprising, then, with regard to issues of climate crisis, that Hayao Miyazaki – when found in the rare, compromising position of having to give answers to questions – has often felt compelled to make comments on the failing relationship between man and nature. Something which, as far back as 2005, led one *New Yorker* writer to dub the director 'an environmentalist... of a somewhat dark and apocalyptic variety,' noting, among other things, a past assertion that he 'looked forward to the time when Tokyo is submerged by the ocean and the NTV tower becomes an island, when the human population plummets and there are no more high-rises.'[1]

Similarly, that Isao Takahata so frequently weighed in on Japanese politics with regard to the country's remilitarisation feels like a natural extension of his work and his life. In an interview from 2015, three years before his own death, Takahata can be found citing the French poet Jacques Prevert: his inversion of a Roman proverb, turning "If you want peace, prepare for war" into "If you don't want war, repair peace" is followed by his own typically succinct summary of the situation. Here, true to his beliefs from beginning to end, he offers: 'You cannot keep the peace by picking up a weapon.'[2]

These, then, are the dual foundations of Studio Ghibli: Takahata's first film for the studio, *Grave of the Fireflies*, being a tale of intimate familial loss amid the shock and awe of all-out war, based on the post-Hiroshima novel *Barefoot Gen*, and the success of Miyazaki's ecological epic, *Nausicaä of the Valley of the Wind*, having acted as the initial impetus for the studio's formation. Just as there is no escape from loss, there is no escaping the fact that Studio Ghibli was built on the notion of grief – perhaps before it even really began.

From then on, they have only expanded and solidified those foundations: the death of childhood, the death of love, the death of our connection to the natural world and our innate ability to see beyond the obvious and into the numinous.

There are griefs for all of these and more across the decades-long breadth of the Ghibli filmography. Sometimes candidly laid out for all to see, as with *Princess Mononoke*'s heart-on-the-sleeve environmental preoccupations where humans are literally at war with nature, and others not so much – as with *Spirited Away*'s nuanced approach to the end of youth, or the ways in which *Howl's Moving Castle* so subtly captures the complex idea of the death of one self and the birth of another in its place through the power of someone else's unconditional love. These are not simple ideas, but they are more or less universal: we all age, we all come to understand ourselves in new ways – sometimes good, sometimes not so much

– and we all live in a world teetering on the brink of ecological disaster.

They are universal truths: yes, they are skilfully embedded in magical narratives which create a degree of distance and apply the veneer of entertainment, but they are no less powerful for that element of fantasy or artistry.

In his novel, *Grief is the Thing with Feathers*, which itself shares more than a few of the archetypal and animistic characteristics so commonplace in Ghibli, Max Porter draws a line between these complex topics – of grief, of the end – and the idea of youth as a natural conduit for such heavy thoughts. 'Ghosts do not haunt, they regress,' he writes. 'Just as when you need to go to sleep you think of trees or lawns, you are taking instant symbolic refuge in a ready-made iconography of early safety and satisfaction. That exact place is where ghosts go.'

That all of this – things and people that are all the time dying; their inevitable final death – is dealt with so thoroughly and so eloquently through a medium that many, correctly or not, would consider to be for younger audiences, then, is perhaps much less surprising than it seems.

In this sense it is important to understand that introducing children to the essential nature of life, that everything – everything good and everything bad;

everything that is and will be – has its own natural end point, is not in any way a callous act. It does not rob them of anything or shatter the precious and precarious illusions of their youth. To understand this and to accept it is a kind of grief in and of itself. A death of something, perhaps, but one that is vital and soft and tender – one for which we should be grateful to be handed as a cushion for the much harder and less graceful falls of the future.

I wrote once about how – unbeknownst to my nine-year-old self – the Pixar movie *Toy Story 2*, which perhaps not unrelatedly and also entirely correctly holds a 100% Certified Fresh rating on the review aggregator *Rotten Tomatoes*, went some way toward fulfilling that need: preparing me on some level for that first real encounter with mortality, three or four years later in an entirely non-descript yet very much unforgettable hospital room. Face to face with the undeniable fact of deadness, kissing the suddenly unwrinkled forehead of my once-grandfather as a single drop of blood, seemingly placed there to anchor the scene in reality, made its way from his mouth to his chin.

Given how I would take that encounter and the effect it would have on the rest of my life well into adulthood – how I cannot, even now, see any object covered by a sheet without thinking of a white-cold hospital room and digging my fingernails into my palms – it's fair to say that it did not go quite as far as I might have needed. Perhaps there was simply too much distance between the idea of a toy cowboy's existential despair, staring down the prospect of ruin at the hands of time, and the notion that this applied to people, too. People that I loved, and to me.

Perhaps, also, it is too much to expect a film for children to take these themes any further, to deal with them any more directly than they do. (Although 1992's *FernGully: The Last Rainforest* certainly instilled in me a very real and very visceral terror about the future of our planet – even if it was the kind of fear which did not stop me from watching that movie on repeat, practically wearing out the VHS, and which came replete with an outstandingly campy vocal performance by the incomparable Tim Curry.) But the films of Studio Ghibli make some effort to close that gap – to treat children and young people as whole human beings, deserving of respect and honesty, but also of care and a gentler touch. They do not need to be lied to – in fact, they can and should be told the entire truth lest they stumble upon that truth themselves and are hurt more deeply than they should have been. Still, the delivery is everything.

There is something else, too. Something – as much as it might seem a strange point of reference in a book about animated movies – perhaps best captured by the writer

Joan Didion in her memoir *Blue Nights*. In that book, aptly dedicated to her daughter Quintana who is also its subject, she makes the observation that 'when we talk about mortality we are talking about our children.'

Thinking about that, I wonder whether so many Ghibli heroes are children not just because children will then relate to them – or even because it is easier to paint them as innocents in the eyes of an audience – but also because, as adults, when we think about death and mortality, we think about children. Whether we have them or not, the two are inextricable – their connection is the realisation of our worst nightmares.

Perhaps that's why, when I dream about death – and I do so frequently – I am not myself as I am right now, in this moment. Instead, inevitably, I am much younger. I am a child.

A child like Mei, or Seita, or Sosuke. Like Chihiro, hounded by a monster with no face – no set identity. Just a thing waiting to happen. Grief, wrapped in a white sheet, hanging back in pause and waiting for its moment; for that anchor to reality.

Chapter 2
Our neighbour, certain death

Call this a sweeping generalisation, or perhaps even a self-own of sorts, but in the West we don't do well with death. As a result of that, we really don't do well with the grief that follows either.

What Benjamin Franklin left out of his pithy but astute observation that 'only two things in life are certain, death and taxes', it seems, is the question of which we're willing to jump through the most hoops to avoid.

Some 230-odd years on, the taxes are certainly gaining ground on that front – in fact, we're getting to the point now where the idiom may well need rewriting – but, in the end, it's still death and grief that we're running from the hardest. Although, inevitably, it's the one we're only ever really running toward.

Everything we do is geared around avoidance, rather than acceptance. Eternal life and bodily resurrection through religion at one end, research into fields such as cryogenics and other science-fiction-made-real endeavours at the other. Even the more innocuous treatments like fillers and Botox, really, are just an attempt to dam the flow of time toward the gaping maw of that dark river mouth.

In short: we're all going to die some time, but nobody really wants to die at any time at all. As a result, life itself is basically one long and futile attempt at self-perpetuation – whether that's in the literal, medical sense, in terms of hanging on to some semblance of youth for as long as possible, or manifested in the things we set out to achieve that might outlast our bodies and keep our names on the lips of the world. Death is all around us, infused into more or less every human endeavour – consciously or otherwise, from art to architecture to the act of having children – because the drive to escape the unavoidable is so powerful. Because of these doomed efforts at immortality, often made in vain but also, admirably, in hope, grief, too, exists in all these things. Regardless of their success by whatever other measure, ultimately, in this one respect they failed, even if they failed beautifully.

It's not just our lives, either, that we dedicate so thoroughly to avoiding death by any means: even death itself, or the process that comes immediately after death, is set-up to remove as much of the reality and finality as possible. Not just in the religious sense: as mortician Caitlin Doughty points out in her book, *Smoke Gets in Your Eyes*, the 20th Century's push toward the "medical-isation" of death, 'removed from view all the gruesome sights, smells, and sounds of death' – essentially puts up a barrier between the realities of dying and death itself.

In that same book, which deals mostly with Doughty's early experiences in the death industry – and, in particular, the lessons learned from her first job at a crematorium – she also quotes the anthropologist Geoffrey Gorer on the same line of thinking: 'In many cases, it would appear, cremation is chosen because it is felt to get rid of the dead more completely and finally than does burial.' This way, with this degree of separation, we are able to disregard the idea of the remnants – the remains – and focus, instead, on the process of arranging memories into remembrances; into a coherent, if not entirely accurate, summary of a person's life and our place within that. Without the fact of a body to complicate things, we are free; free to do the essential work of reassembling the person we have lost in a way that makes sense. In a way that we, as the ones left behind, can live with.

These pieces of the person are mostly metaphorical – psychic and emotional, logistical even.

And thus, we return to Studio Ghibli by way of Caitlin Doughty. Recalling an incident from her youth and the knock-on effects of that event, still seemingly clacking on like a grim Newton's Cradle to this day, even if a little less quickly and a little less loudly, she writes, 'Sometimes I think of how my childhood would have been different if I had been introduced directly to death. Made to sit in his presence, shake his hand… Maybe he would have been a friend.'

Perhaps not just a friend, but a neighbour.

*

In 1988, Studio Ghibli released *My Neighbor Totoro* – a film that more or less perfectly, and certainly more than any other animated picture that I can think of, captures what it is and what it means to live alongside death and grief.

To explain that film here, in isolation – wherein two young girls move to an old house in the Japanese countryside with their father, befriending an enormous forest troll, his fun-sized troll friends, and a cat which is also a bus – I realise that it sounds an unlikely candidate for something so intense; something which sounds, on the face of it, so dark. But, firstly, that top-line summary is missing some important detail. And, secondly, that immediate association – of death with darkness; of grief

24

with despair and the void – is not the way in which this film, or Ghibli in general, approaches the nature of human mortality.

So, then, what is that missing detail? It's not just that dear-old-dad is going it alone and giving it his best shot – Adam Sandler in *Big Daddy* he very much is not. No, in this particular story, with its upbeat theme and cast of whimsical characters, dad is in charge because the kids' mother is in the midst of yet another long hospital stay; suffering with some unspecified but clearly Not Great illness, unable to return home for fear of the risk that her condition might deteriorate even further.

Now, if this particular set-up sounds familiar, that's because it is. Miyazaki has often said that the strong women in his films are based – however loosely – on aspects of his own mother's personality; but, in the case of Mei and Satsuki in *Totoro*, the mother figure is hardly removed from the one in Miyazaki's life at all.

Despite the apparent and increasing graveness of her condition, the film ends with the girls' mother well enough to return to the family in their new home some time soon. Against all the odds, she makes it through to the final frame alive, if not entirely well. It's a "happy ending" of sorts that, in a particularly ungenerous inter-pretation, could easily be misread as a kind of fairy tale cop-out. But this unlikely trajectory isn't a Disneyfication of a harsh reality — it's a direct parallel to the director's own story. Miyazaki's mother, despite being in and out of hospital for much of his childhood, and then nursed from home for much of the rest of her life, lived until the age of seventy-two.

More than this, beyond the intrigue of the auto-biographical note, there is something substantial about this narrative on a broader, more universally human level. That the mother character (and Yoshiko Miyazaki avatar) in *Totoro* lives is an even more vital lesson — a more necessary story.

Death and grief stalk every frame of this film, walking in tandem with Mei and Satsuki and their father, and anyone else whose life their own impacts upon. That there is no jump scare, no *Bambi* or *Lion King*-esque moment of bleak gratification, wherein all our worst fears are realised, is not an evasion but a potent storytelling device, one which says: "There is no closure here — no endpoint. Things are simply not that easy." It says that death, as much of a contradiction as it seems, isn't an event; it isn't something that just *happens*: it's something you have to learn to live with. Not just once, as an unnamed monster that will disappear off into the night once the deed is done, but forever. An eternal phantom — neither benev-olent nor benign, but not inherently evil either.

Just a spectre, a poltergeist. A presence which, once seen, cannot be unseen. And one which only grows more powerful – only becomes angry or violent, like a petulant child – with each flimsy attempt at feigning ignorance.

Given the peculiar subject matter of this book, its two main threads, there's something I want to go ahead and get out of the way early: what we're talking about here has nothing to do with the misguided idea of Totoro – title character of one of Ghibli's most enduring works, warmly laconic and endearingly narcoleptic friend to the children Mei and Satsuki Kusakabe – as a Japanese Shinigami spirit. Essentially, a God of Death.

Enticing as it might be as a fan theory, this is a pop-culture folktale of sorts – a kind of anime urban myth. *My Neighbor Totoro* is many things – moving, empathetic, put together with characteristic beauty and attention to detail – but an animated version of M. Night Shyamalan's *The Sixth Sense* it is most certainly not. The children of *Totoro* the film are not suddenly able to perceive and interact with Totoro the character because they are themselves no longer alive – because they have now moved on to his ethereal plane. That, as they say, *just ain't it*.

But debunking this curious little myth does not mean that death isn't present in the film or that Totoro the figure does not have a key role to play in that representation. It doesn't even mean that the benign forest troll – planter of seeds, sharer of umbrellas – is not himself a totem, an archetype, or an avatar for grief. He may not be the bringer of death – that interpretation can stay on *Reddit*, where, ironically enough, people just won't let it die – but perhaps there is some truth to the idea that Mei and Satsuki stumble upon Totoro precisely because of what, to them, must surely feel like a lingering malevolence. Because they need Totoro in their lives; as a protector of sorts, but more than anything as a guide to living in this world under the cloud of mortality. As a friendly reminder that death, while imminent and tangible, also has its own transformative magic.

Or, perhaps, Totoro – while still not a demon or a death god – is actually a manifestation of Death itself: for Mei and Satsuki, he and his miniature compatriots – with their out of control acorn habit and skittish nature – may be a real-life rendering of a force in their lives that cannot be ignored so easily as either they or their father would like to believe.

When the totoro creatures are first revealed to the girls, it's something of a gradual process: clear yet unfamiliar footsteps in the ground, fading in and out of reality – something that is not of this world, but which is definitely, unassailably, *there*. While I realise that it may be an unlikely point of reference, it's a scene which always puts me in mind of what I consider to be one of T.S. Eliot's most affecting lines from *The Waste Land*.

Taken from 'What the Thunder Said', and reportedly inspired by Ernest Shackleton's desperate (and very nearly doomed) Antarctic voyage of 1914-17, Eliot asks: 'Who is the third who walks always beside you? / When I count, there are only you and I together / But when I look ahead up the white road / There is always another one walking beside you.'

In his account, taken from his own book, *South*, Shackleton talks about the "third man" in describing an extra, incorporeal member of his party whom he describes as helping them to carry the load and ensure their survival. Eliot, while referencing Shackleton, was likely alluding to something more broad, as he was often – and often much, much less coherently – wont to do. Something slightly more universal than an apparition on the tundra. Something not so different from acorns scattered on the ground, from a bus which is also a cat, from soot gremlins thundering around the corners of an old house, or even from a troll at the bus stop in the rain.

These are all things which seem strange at first – unreal, even, but they are things which the children of *My Neighbor Totoro* learn, quickly and keenly, to accept as a fact of their uncertain lives. Cumulatively – and in their most complete and final form as the largest and most recognisable of these creatures – the various magical beings of *Totoro* comprise the "Third" to Mei and Satsuki's sisterly pairing. Arriving always and only at the moments they're most needed – helping the two girls to carry a load that is far too heavy for anyone so young.

In one of *Totoro*'s most memorable scenes, soundtracked to perfection by the composer and frequent Ghibli collaborator Joe Hisaishi, the more-often docile Big Totoro leads the human children in a kind of ritualistic dance. Together – along with his miniature, magical compatriots – they take the laws of nature into their own hands, turning seeds into full-grown trees before their eyes.

It is a particularly beautiful and evocative scene, and one which says as much as anything about the attitude of this film and of Studio Ghibli as a whole toward death and grieving. While the mighty oaks the group had conjured by darkness have disappeared by day, there is something that remains. There in the dirt, there are sprouts. The tiny green shoots of hope and possibility. A message that while there is death, there is also life and a reminder, too, that grief is not known for its brevity: that life, as we know it, does not simply resume overnight in the glow of the stars and the moon. That when the sun comes up again, and it will, things may still be wrong, but there may be signs of better things to come.

It's not just in *Totoro* (or in Totoro, for that matter) that we find grief so vividly manifested. Elsewhere, there are other totems – other embodiments and incarnations littering the Ghibli filmography, from cats to fireflies to talking flames. Among all of them, the stand-out and the star – the cover star in this case, even – is No-Face, the melancholy, black-and-white-masked troublemaker of *Spirited Away*.

In many ways, No-Face (who, in the original Japanese, is referred to as Kaonashi – "Faceless") has much in common with Totoro. Granted, No-Face has a slightly more sinister appearance and some questionable ideas about what constitutes an appropriate way of making friends, but there are more parallels than there are differences.

Kaonashi only shows up at the bath house of the spirits shortly after Chihiro has stumbled her own way into that world. After her parents have been taken from her – now stuck somewhere between life and death in the form of squealing pigs – she works her way toward setting them free whilst also being forced to accept that they may well be gone from her life forever, and suddenly No-Face makes an appearance with eyes for no one else.

It's a little less cute and fluffy than Mei and Satsuki's meeting with Totoro – which is funny, really, given that the narrative content of *Spirited Away* is a little more on the magical end of the scale – where even if the threat of peril to Chihiro and her parents feels more constant and more present, the stakes seem somehow lower. Not because the storytelling is any less dramatic or engaging, but – probably, in no small part – because hospitals and illness and death by natural causes are very real, very tangible and unavoidable parts of life. Parental pigs and spa-owning witches with a penchant for child labour, not so much.

Still, the similarities remain, from the fact that, early on in the film No-Face only appears to Chihiro, down to much smaller details such as the way in which this curiously legless spirit somehow manages to leave a set of spectral footprints when he floats incognito about the place; a trail by which to be discovered, hiding in plain sight.

It is also the ways in which Kaonashi is distinctly not like Totoro, too, which mark him as an emissary for death and grief.

The ways in which he hounds Chihiro through the spirit world: how quickly he moves from his first appearances as a faint, translucent phantom to a vivid, monochromatic form; how his presence overwhelms not only Chihiro, or even the other spirits of the bath house, but also the very story of *Spirited Away* – taking over from the main narrative arc and literally devouring the world around her until she has no choice but to engage. How his facelessness speaks of a void, and how he hungrily absorbs the life-force of anything and everything in his way. All of these things are what we think of when we think of death. They are also the same elements which constitute the very nature of grief – the complex and unwieldy effects it has on those whom it touches, and who have no say in whether or not it is a touch to which they consent.

In No-Face we are shown that grief, like death, does not wait for an invitation; that it does not leave the party upon finding out that one was never issued in the first place, only becoming more irate, more out of control, and more all-consuming with every attempt to push it out the door. But in that same character, we are also shown something else – something typically Miyazaki: not only the futility but also the wrongheadedness of those attempts. That Chihiro eventually befriends Kaonashi – returned to a state of bodily transparency and low-key melancholy – and is pushed to confront the predicament of her parents' mortal danger head-on, is a fairly clear aide-memoire from the director. A note, for those who need reminding – which I think it would be fair to say is all of us, to some degree or another – that ignoring our problems does not make them go away. It allows them to fester and expand, somewhere out of shot, until the moment at which they have become so large and so putrid that their presence is not only unavoidable by virtue of their size, but also much more difficult to deal with in terms of the strength which they have gathered.

When it comes to something as significant as grief, this only becomes more true.

Again, though, there is hope of a sort.

As is always the case with Miyazaki, it is a kind of hope that does not come for free. It is a hope which requires something, not necessarily a sacrifice, per se, but a decision. The way in which Kaonashi is so thoroughly tamed – in one scene, now so helpless against even the smallest of lapping waves that his sighing lament has become a popular reaction meme for moments of emotional overwhelm – kindly offers up the key to understanding that decision.

It is only after Chihiro has gone toe-to-toe with No-Face at his absolute worst – screaming, frenzied and gigantic, foaming at the mouth – that he is quelled into submission; only after he is seen as the monster he is capable of being that he is reduced to something far less frightening. Only after all of this, all of this violence and trauma, does Kaonashi – in his diminutive state – become not an enemy to Chihiro but a friend. A silent passenger on a long train journey, taking up space but doing no harm. A familiar face, even if one with no face at all to speak of.

When, early in the film, Chihiro first sees the spectral No-Face – hovering outside of the bath house, looking by all counts pretty spooky – and then decides, instead of

34

hiding, to leave a door open so that he can come in from the rain, she has the right idea. It's one that, lost somewhere in all the commotion and the fear, she'll spend much of *Spirited Away* working her own way back to.

For Chihiro, as with anyone in the whirling throes and jolting convulsions of loss, it takes time to see what was right in front of her all along: to realise that making an enemy of grief is only ever a diversion. That, in seeing it as a battle, or something she can work her way out of in some other way, she only begins an unwinnable war of attrition with the inescapable. In *Spirited Away*, it takes Chihiro so long to realise this not because she is a child or even because it makes for a better narrative arc, but because it *is* a hard thing with which to come to terms: to accept the fact that this thing – this enormous, monstrous thing – is not something to be beaten, not something you can fight or atone for through hard, mindless labour. The truth is that it is hard to cede control – painful in its own way, another kind of loss in itself, but it is also necessary. It may feel like it at first, but this isn't capitulation – it isn't giving up, it's something more like giving in.

Sometimes, giving in is the best option there is to find a way out.

*

My Neighbor Totoro wasn't the only film that Ghibli released in 1988. That's the benefit of having two of animation's best, most thoughtful, and most belligerent directors on your staff. In tandem with Miyazaki's complex but lighthearted take on love and loss came Isao Takahata's treatise on the same: *Grave of the Fireflies*.

A very different film to its release-schedule partner, *Grave* tells the story of teenage Seita and his much younger sister Setsuko, following them in their lives after their home is destroyed at the tail-end of World War Two. It is, and I cannot stress this enough, a much harder watch than *Totoro*. The kind of film you just shouldn't watch at all if you aren't emotionally prepared and have nothing left to do that day but sleep it off.

Despite what the two films do share – on the face of it, both coming of age stories, young children left behind, in part, to fend for themselves under a cloud of grief and uncertainty – the catharsis of *Grave*, if you can call it that, though rooted in the same conclusions as *Totoro*, is not by any means a joyful one.

Not long after we meet Seita and Setsuko, the pair of siblings are quickly orphaned by a brutal and wholly unnecessary air raid on their largely peaceful village – a sharp parallel to the atrocities committed against real-world Japan that very same year. You'd be forgiven for thinking that things can only get better. Here, there is only a long, winding, descent – one that only gives us hope in order to quickly snatch it out from under us, where the elements of fantasy are conspirators in the dark depths of the film's beleaguering realism.

Without going into too much detail of the plot, things do not go well for either older brother or younger sister. Cut loose from their lives, they are forced to build a new one together: a world wherein the gaping holes of their new reality – lack of food, proper shelter and clean water – are patched in-part by make believe.

Writing about *Grave* back in 2018 – the year the film turned thirty and the year its director, Isao Takahata, passed away from lung cancer – I wrote again about my grandfather, and about the night he died. About the similarities in the way that Seita and Setsuko's story is told and then untold – so clear at first, but ultimately lost in the murk of time and loss.

Searching for something more than the run-of-the-mill death of two old men with run-of-the-mill cancers to link these things together, I dredged the depths of my memories and came up with both more and less than I had hoped for: incongruous recollections, lined up and heaped upon each other, like artefacts of a time gone by – some entirely incompatible with others, but none, to my mind, any less correct or less real than the others.

Parallel histories, written and rewritten to make sense of a story that just did not add up for me back then.

Writing in *The Quietus*, I first made this admission to myself: 'I may not remember the first time I watched *Grave of the Fireflies* exactly and, in truth, I have not watched it again until I came to write this. I do, however, remember the night my grandfather died, in excruciating detail, having played it back innumerable times in my head since then. Or, at least, I tell myself that I do…

'As time passes and cracks open, however, I have to ask myself if the minutiae I have clung to for so long now represent anything but an attempt to hold, white-knuckle tight, on to smoke in the open air. Were the lights in that small room or the colour of his skin quite as grey as I remember? Was either actually as cold?'[1]

In truth, the more I grimaced, gritted my teeth, and thought back to that night, the less sure I became of anything. Sometimes, now, I even forget the date – confuse my own age at the time it all happened, or finished happening. But this is not about what is real and what is not – about truths ignored and lies told. At this point, almost twenty years later, it is all true. Every wrong number, errant sound, image or smell is as much gospel to me as the ones which an objective observer might recall as "correct".

There was no objective observer then. There never is. There is no way, even on the periphery, to be a party to grief and not have it confound your senses and your sense of the world.

What about that catharsis I mentioned earlier – how can all of this uncertainty and all of these questions add up to anything at all? The answer, really, is that they don't – but that's okay. There is nothing to be gained from forcing the pieces together, because – as with Seita and Setsuko's fantasy world – whatever you build will be fragile and far from built to last.

As a final thought in that essay, I wrote that *Grave* is something like 'a soft-focus snapshot of an unreliably faded photograph: as adherent conceptually in form to the complex intertwining of memory and of grief as possible, emblematic of the distortions we impose – wilfully or otherwise – to get by on a daily basis.'[2]

What *Grave of the Fireflies* shows us is not just what it means to live a lie, or to live through a lie, but also what it means to die for one – to commit so thoroughly to the fantasy that it becomes all consuming, consumptive. What it asks us is where that line is drawn and whether it is ever really drawn at all.

For my part, I cannot wholly escape these distortions, regardless of whether or not I can certify their provenance. I cannot undo the time I have spent with them. But knowing this, at least, brings a certain kind of freedom to live. The possibility that I might one day do something as simple as watch the film *Little Miss Sunshine* without drawing blood from the palms of my hands with my fingernails at the sight of the old man's body under that sheet.

Not a guarantee, but – yes – a chance. I'll take that.

*

Maybe it's worth mentioning here that *Spirited Away* was the first title I suggested for this book. At the time, it made perfect sense. Now that I think about it, I'm glad it is not. I chose *Spirited Away* for the obvious reasons, but now that I've had time to sit here and think about those reasons they just don't sit right anymore.

This is a book about grief – about things which happen that do not necessarily make sense but which we must make sense of in order to move on in at least some small way. *Spirited Away* – although, yes, replete with all the ghostly connotations and the implications of what's left behind – suggests something intangible; something not of this world; something which, in its lightness of touch, just *kind of happens*, but that isn't what grief is like. Not really. As a title, *Spirited Away* would only reinforce all of the things I am trying here – and have been trying for so long in my own life up until this point – to break down: the idea that death and loss and grief are distant things – like stars, blinking in the night sky, beautiful but ultimately already faded from existence. That name would have been an easy way out: just another way of avoiding the truth. Another fantasy, blended indiscriminately with reality, deployed only with a view to dissolving any distinction between the two – as if that membrane weren't already permeably and porous enough.

But grief is real; it's physical – it doesn't just happen, or even happen *to* you. It is there. Right there. Next to you, always. Only when you have sat together long enough, had enough altercations and conversations, left open enough doors and walked through them together can you decide that you'd like some time alone.

Only then, so close and so intimate, can you feel free to ask for a reprieve. To say, "Now Go."

Chapter 3
The squandered gift

Some things are inevitable.

Death is inevitable. Loss too. Change – good or bad, like it or not, in one form or another – is inevitable. Things tomorrow will be different from how they are today. Inevitability itself is a part of life. It is, in a sense, the only real constant.

What is not quite so certain, though, is the way we reach that conclusion and how that is applied to our view of the world; how we arrive at acceptance and which things, exactly, we have the choice to accept. Because some things are not so inevitable as they appear. Some things which we readily accept as fact are, instead, more like convenient fictions.

But convenient for whom, exactly?

*

I wrote that truth and innocence are not mutually exclusive. That shielding the young from grief is not necessarily the best way to make sure that they continue to see the beauty in life. That, though it might seem like a kindness, you simply can't keep these things hidden forever; they are too large, too looming to be confined to the periphery. What's more, they are too shocking when they appear as if from nowhere rather than eased in to focus over time. There is a tenderness to truth which may at first seem so sharp as to be counterintuitive but which, in the long run, dulls the blade of loss through regularity of use.

Acceptance, though, is not the same as defeat; and loss, of course, is not by any means confined to youth. There is a through line: a thread which runs – from cradle to grave, so to speak – of incremental loss, of daily griefs so small as to be almost imperceptible. Losses which it is easier to accept than to fight; easier to ignore than to rally against or to question.

As every day passes, the machinations of the world in which we live take without giving in return – gears grind on and, in doing so, grind down. In response to this, with age, we develop a way to protect ourselves: a certain kind of denialism – something more akin to cynicism – which runs like stodgy, half-coagulated blood through the veins

44

of the fully grown. A sense, which can be hard to shake, whispering in our ears that to live in this world is to live in the world exactly as it is right now; that nothing can change. That nothing needs to change. That the concrete facts of life – social, political, economic – are all that there is to it.

While we might reason that accepting this is just another form of insulation against the shock of inevitable reality, it is not the same as – say – acknowledging the nature of our fleeting existence. It is a step beyond that. A step too far, even. And one from which it is much more difficult to step backward once taken.

It is also a step which Studio Ghibli constantly asks us to reconsider. Whether through allusions to the nature, the futility, and the toll of labour with films like *Spirited Away*, or to the weight of existing within – and I hate to say it – a society with characters like the downtrodden Sophie Hatter of *Howl's Moving Castle*, Miyazaki often seems to be giving us a gentle nudge toward pulling our heads out of the sand, or wherever else they might be located. A nudge to consider our place within the world as it is and within the systems that rule it. Telling us that something concrete is by no means indestructible, nor should it be thought of as such.

In short, that the world, and the way it treats us – the systems which coerce us to change ourselves in order to comply and comfortably exist within their seemingly immutable structures – can be changed instead. Or, if not, that we are free to exist outside of them. That the route to happiness and fulfilment is found in circumventing those systems.

That it comes, instead, from within.

*

Oftentimes, in art as much as simply in life, there is a sense that the fundamental difference between adults and children is the loss of one thing and the gaining of another. I'm not going to wade into religion here – not least of all because I personally have none, and absolutely zero skin in the came when it comes to such things – but the way in which Philip Pullman renders this distinction tangible in the form of something that he calls Dust has always stuck with me.

Dust is a mysterious substance, invisible to the naked eye and acquired through puberty, clinging to children only as they begin their transition to young adults – it signifies the loss of "innocence" at the hands of experience, which in Pullman's *His Dark Materials* trilogy is a way of explaining how the young, through no fault of their own, end up shouldering the burden and the guilt of Original Sin.

I mention this here because, while I neither believe in dust nor Original Sin, there are enough parallels to a reality where neither need be accepted as fact for it to still make a worthy comparison. Perhaps there is a certain kind of magic in the world only perceptible with the benefit of a child's – or, at least, child-like – freedom. Whether that magic is supernatural or not, it is certainly a gift, one which we are all-too-willing to squander: out of ignorance, laziness, or just a failure to hold on to a peculiar curiosity which dims quickly and dies with the years if underused. Perhaps most curiously and undoubtedly sad of all, it can be out of some form of embarrassment – a desire not to be perceived as someone who does not "understand" the ways of the world or the socialised version of adulthood which we are groomed to accept. To, in other words, just "fit in".

Little by little, our wonder at the world around us evaporates over time, condensing into the cold steam of disillusionment. Most of these small erosions go unchecked; it's only their cumulative effect that kicks in and eventually kicks our asses as a people and a population en masse when the edges finally begin to crumble and slide into the abyss.

Examining all of this – the ways in which we, as people, change over time into fully-formed adults with a shared idea of what it is that adults should do, or how they should act – also means considering why we ascribe certain things to child-like behaviours even when the things themselves have not changed at all. Why should something like the rain, to cite just one recent example provided to us by the emotionally unguarded Drew Barrymore, be a near-miracle through the eyes of a child but considered nothing more than an inconvenience to an adult on pain of derision?

The world works hard to beat out of us the things about which we care the most – to dilute our passions and temper our reactions. The world at large, to its great shame, is scornful of people who live deeply. And that scorn is not just a benign clucking of the tongue. It is white-hot and razor sharp. It is painful and precise enough to leave not just a lasting sting but also, if not properly treated, a permanent scar of self-doubt: a reminder to think again before exposing yourself to a world in which the done thing is to simply bury the light of those feelings until they are extinguished by a lack of air.

But, again, *why?* Why squeeze the life out of – well – life? To what end, exactly? Why does it hurt you to see the joy in others; hurt enough, even, to want to stomp it out rather than to look? No-one is making you. No-one is asking you for anything. Why not just leave it be? What, really, is the perceived threat here?

It's a complex question – and certainly more complex than the immediate answer it brings to mind: that people are assholes and this is just another example of them being assholes – but it also one which several of

Miyazaki's movies can guide us on, providing insight if not exactly antidote. Deftly, in so many of his directorial offerings, Miyazaki makes clear the foolishness of polarising, to paraphrase William Blake, the concepts of innocence and experience – highlights the mistake in equating knowledge with enlightenment – and shows us that understanding the world need not come at the cost of appreciating it.

*

First released in 1989 – almost a decade before the English-language dub appeared courtesy of the Walt Disney Company – *Kiki's Delivery Service* (or, *Majo no Takkyūbin*, literally: 'Witch's Express Home Delivery') makes for an interesting parable in this sense. One, in many ways, not all too dissimilar to Pullman's – if a little more light-hearted on the surface and a little less prone to mortal peril.

On the top line, *Kiki's* is the story of a young witch who comes of age and leaves home, along with her talking cat Jiji, to start a new life in a new town: at thirteen, she is no longer a child under whatever rules it is that witches are expected to follow here, and the trainee is keen to stake her claim and hone her craft away from the comfort of her family. It's the done thing, and she's enthusiastic about doing it.

When Kiki leaves her hometown and heads for the big city, she is less than capable when it comes to navigating her way there – all wide-eyes and full of wonderment, not so much the competent captain of a broom.

Her parents are proud, if not more than a little worried. Jiji is acerbic and dismissive; a little shit, really. Off they go. Not entirely smoothly or without incident, but off nonetheless, arriving a day or so later at the very handsome and very large port city of Koriko where the thirteen year old Kiki goes about the task of finding herself a job. I'm sure you can guess what happens next. Or, at least, what kind of job she gets. (It's delivering stuff, okay? Stuff for a bakery. Pies. Bread. Bakery things!)

On the face of it, it's all going pretty well. Our young witch has room, board, and a little extra spending money. She's also struggling to fit in: finding it hard to make friends; when the opportunity does present itself, she finds it equally hard to actually even want to. She's a country girl in the big city. She's also a *witch* – something which I, personally, would have found extremely cool – but neither of these things quite tessellate properly with the cosmopolitan social lives of the young people Kiki meets in Koriko.

She perseveres with her newfound vocation. She makes her deliveries, she becomes tired and morose – jaded, even, with the process of putting her incredible talents to good use ferrying bread through the sky. She still has her talking cat, so she's not entirely alone. Except that – somewhere in the middle of this movie – Jiji stops being the little shit we've come to know and love. Not because he's seen the error of his ways, but because he's stopped speaking entirely - or, to Kiki, at least. To make matters worse, she's lost whatever tenuous grip she had on flying that broomstick, too. Essentially, she finds herself not so much a witch with a mouthy familiar and an enchanted mode of transport, but just a girl with a cat, who now only has the regular bad attitude of which every cat is in possession, and also a regular broom – which is useful, but not that interesting.

Everything she knew about herself – that made her special and made the world around her so enchanted – has, cruelly, senselessly, been taken away. No explanation, only the laughter of those other children, considerably more "grown up" in the traditional sense, ringing in her ears.

It is, I have to say, a colossal bummer.

But Miyazaki – even if the source material isn't quite his own, in this case coming from a 1985 novel of the same name – is a steady hand on the tiller. As a director, he's what you might call "firm but fair": even though he rarely condescends to explain the "meaning" of his work in any great detail – possessed of that same penchant for deliberate opacity as the equally inimitable David Lynch – and prefers, instead, to talk about depth in terms of literal imagery, it is rarely the case that he is cruel without reason. He may put his characters through the wringer, but his intentions in doing so are never malicious. So, you have to wonder: what did Kiki ever do to Hayao Miyazaki?

The answer, of course, is nothing. That's the point.

There is no real, obvious antagonist in *Kiki's Delivery Service* – no evil witch or sorcerer, as with so many other of the Ghibli films – who is easily identifiable as the source of Kiki's many woes. The stakes may feel somewhat lower – this is not a film which thrives on life or death tension – and the wretched peril that befalls Kiki is not itself supernatural; quite the opposite, really. What feels, on the face of it, somewhat less dramatic a set-up than with some of its peers, is actually more scathing and more cutting for its low-key narrative: what comes for Kiki – and throws her world into gloomy disarray – is the weight of crushing normality. Instead of a campy, cloak-swishing villain, the "bad guy" here is life and what it does to people who are special – people who are different.

There is also something more specific, too. It is no coincidence that Kiki's troubles begin, not when she leaves the safety net of her parental home, but when she is put to work. Jiji stops talking to her and begins to spend all of his time with another cat; her broom is suddenly only good for sweeping up flour from the bakery which now cakes all of her belongings in an ashy residue. The magic only drains from her life – when the young witch focuses less on the art of witchcraft and what sets her apart from the other residents of Koriko, and more on her assimilation into society. A society which, not to get all undergraduate Marxism about it, is defined and ruled – much like the real world – by the machinations of Capitalism, an ideology which rewards consistency and productivity toward the means of generating value, but which punishes exceptionalism and creativity, refusing to acknowledge their own, innate value.

In short: it's hard to fly – or even to want to – when the world is standing on your neck.

For what it's worth, though, Kiki does recover her broom-flying skills – but only by re-embracing her less ordinary traits. Jiji, though, as far as we know, never speaks again.

That magic, it seems, is lost forever. While there is a school of thought, which says – not too dissimilarly to the ways in which the daemon familiars of Pullman's trilogy only take a final shape post-puberty – that having now fully "grown up", Kiki no longer *needs* to chat with her feline counterpart, it is not a choice she is ever given the opportunity to make for herself. Instead, it is handed to her as a cold, hard fact of life – a loss, reshaping her entire view of the world and her own position within it, for which she was not properly prepared.

*

Having arrived here via chapters on loss in the more traditional sense, I appreciate that perhaps there is something which feels less potent about what you're reading here. "Where," you may be wondering, "is the grief?" I understand that, though I would encourage you to persist here.

When I say that life, in a sense, is a series of petites morts, this is not – unfortunately – as salacious as it sounds. (We can only hope.) Rather, we face a loss of some kind most days and some are smaller than others. Not so much a series of little deaths, then, as little griefs: petits chagrins. We lose time, we lose love, we lose passion, we lose sight of who we are in the shadow of a world which – for the most part, at least – does not care to know the eccentricities of our inner workings, or wish for us to wear them on our sleeves.

As is often the case when it comes to condensing complex feelings into beautiful, truncated verse, Frank O'Hara perhaps said it best – this time in 'Mayakovsky', from 1975's *Meditations in an Emergency* when he spoke of the diminishing returns of being alive in this world – about waiting for his sense of self, the catastrophe of his personality as he so aptly put it, to seem beautiful again in the face of an ever-dulling life.

If this, this constantly fading lustre, isn't an articulation of loss – if this, right here, isn't grief – then I don't know what is. It is not always death itself, in the way which we imagine, hooded and skeletal, that puts its bony fingers on the fragile flame of our being and stirs in us that rending feeling – in part because, sometimes, we do not feel it at all until it is far too late. But it is always a death of some kind, one which we only notice when accompanied by the tell-tale hiss and the foreboding dark that follows.

*

Naturally, I am not the first person to write about Hayao Miyazaki's distaste for capitalist culture and the trappings which necessarily come with it – there's just too much material here for that common thread to go unnoticed for this long. An article from Harvard University's paper, *The Crimson*, tends to agree.

In her piece from late-2021, writer Bella Kim goes as far as to call the Oscar-winning *Spirited Away* a 'Timeless Tale of Capitalism', which is not the romanticisation it might sound like. '*Spirited Away*,' Kim writes, 'is a meticulously-crafted criticism of Westernization and capitalism, a story advocating for a restoration of and respect for the traditional… in contrast to the common modern blind dive for growth and advancement.'

Of all the countless readings of the complex and multi-layered film, it may not be the most engaging or magical — but it's also not wrong.

We've already been through *Spirited Away* – parents, pigs, job at the bath house; you remember – but, in this context, perhaps it bears repeating: among other things, Chihiro is told that the only way she can rectify her unusual and entirely supernatural predicament is through painstaking and considerably less magical hard labour. To don a uniform, both literal and figurative, and to work her way out of the problem.

First, she loses her parents, then she loses her autonomy – and, in effect, her childhood. Not just to the foul-tempered witch Yubaba, whom she now serves, but also to the master which Yubaba in turn defers to: money. In the process, Chihiro gives up her freedom and her name – a name which, over time, she begins to forget.

That, when Chihiro does find her way out of the bath house and out of the world of the spirits, replete with parents – back in human form and with seemingly no recollection of their squealing and slop-guzzling – she does so not through work but through such intangibles as "love" and "friendship" is about as clear a statement as one can make. A testament to what Miyazaki clearly considers to be the correct hierarchy of values – the one we deserve, but also the one which, he often seems to tell us, we do not fight quite hard enough to protect, at least, not until it's too late.

Grief – for a life that was or a life that could have been – is a powerful motivator.

In an article for the website *Cracked*, William Kuechenberg takes things a step further: in a piece titled 'Every Studio Ghibli Film is Secretly About the Same Thing,' he defines that one thing as 'the conflict between everything that's true, good, and beautiful in the world … and capitalism.'[1]

Now, whether that's quite as true and quite as clear-cut as it seems in the title is a matter for debate, but there is a line that can be traced through at the very least most of the Ghibli filmography – and certainly when those films are attributed to Miyazaki, a man who, despite my earlier self-effacing jibes about student politics, considers – or has, at various points in his life, considered – himself to be a Marxist at heart. Perhaps, more accurately, a Marxist *with* heart.

'The ongoing motif of his films,' Kuechenberg continues, 'is that capitalism saps the wonderment from the world and leads to the spiritual diminishment of humanity': a piece of commentary with which it's difficult to argue against – either when it comes to the films of Hayao Miyazaki, or when taken at face value.

While the article deals with more than just *Spirited Away* – it does identify the film as perhaps the most obviously, overtly, anti-capitalist piece of work in the Ghibli filmography, connecting that Chihiro's new name – "Sen", which translates as "One Thousand" – is not a name at all, but a number, to Miyazaki's own assertion that "we lose feelings of reality when we work for the numbers."

It's an idea backed up throughout the film – not least of all in the fact that No-Face, swollen to monstrous proportions and swallowing people whole along with ludicrous amounts of food, is only able to be calmed and returned to a more docile state of being when lured away from the bath house; away from the gold – which, somewhat on the nose, turns out to be a kind of fool's gold – he is hoarding and using to feed a bottomless and entirely senseless greed with which the spirit himself has no personal connection.

Poor Kaonashi is the literal face of the faceless worker – driven not by desire, but by a perpetual motion engineered by forces beyond his control. He is battered and beaten. Broken, even. His attempts at ending the cycle by playing its game having failed, his freedom and fulfilment are eventually found not through work – not even through the ultimate capitalist goal of money which makes money without the need for labour – but through those same intangible qualities which also break Chihiro's chains.

Love might not be all you need, but perhaps it ought to be. Love and loss – loss, which pushes us to ask questions. To query the necessity of what is given up and to ask whether anything is returned in its place. The kinds of questions which, ironically, were it not for another kind of loss, we would not need pushing to ask in the first place.

*

All this self-realisation, too, presents a kind of loss. An almost a never-ending cycle of sorts.

After all, it is all well and good to point to the ways in which the machinations of our culture – and the spread of Western culture, in particular – have failed and continue to fail us on an almost daily basis. It is all very well, too, to suggest that the only way of undoing these failures is to denounce the system and replace it with something else. Something, ideally speaking, better and more spiritually enriching, but the solutions here, admittedly, are vague – they are airy and conceptual. They have more to do with that 'restoration of the traditional' which Kim observes, rather than something new or which can be applied on any real scale.

More, in essence, to do with what can, should, or will be lost than what there is to be gained. More to do with the things for which, ultimately, we should grieve than things for which we should strive.

Maybe that's because – in Miyazaki's eyes – those things, that magic, are already here. Right in front of us. Perhaps, we ought not to be looking for new solutions when we are staring the most incredible gift horse in the mouth – even as we destroy it.

There is hope, though. The irony is that we – each of us – has had it all along. Sometimes buried deep, almost inaccessible, but there nonetheless. It isn't easy to reach, especially when our hands are slapped away for even beginning that motion, but to endure the sting of those raps is to find something well worth the pain. Over time, it's a pain which disappears – leaving only that raw nerve of joy. Leaving only the wonder which has, once again, taken solid form in a world that feels a little brighter. A little less mundane. A whole lot more alive.

Chapter 4
The animated anthropocene

"The Earth speaks to all of us, and if we listen, we can understand." – *Castle in the Sky*

As I sit here writing this, breaking the fourth wall in the process, a satellite image of the United Kingdom is circulating on social media. It is, in many ways, a familiar image: having lived here more or less consistently for over thirty years at this point, it would be strange to say otherwise. For better or for worse – and it is often worse – I can recognise, if nothing else, the outline of this country and its various constituent parts from the low-orbit space of a weather satellite. In other ways, the image is strange: we are experiencing a heatwave – another heatwave, actually – and this image shows a vision not only of that present-day temperature, but also of a possible future.

A likely future, one where grasslands have given up the ghost of verdancy and consigned themselves instead to a state of flaxen combustibility. It has been some time now since anyone could – with any sense of sincerity – refer to England's "green and pleasant land" as William Blake, who it is worth mentioning also thought that the devil had appeared to him in a tree, once did. Until very recently, we could still call it green.

There is a deep magic within our innate sense of self, but an even deeper magic of our connection to the planet on which we play out our lives, day-to-day – living, even as it slowly dies. Actually – less passive, more violent and more detrimental: we are choking its life, so that we might continue to live in the ways to which we have become accustomed. For now, while it lasts. To say this ought not be contentious: it is a matter of science – proven science.

The price of inaction – or of movement in the wrong direction – is something which the directors of Studio Ghibli seem not just to understand but, characteristically, rally against on firebrand form: they may not exactly have The Answers – but they do, with an unusual clarity and deeply-felt sense of certain, see the problems at hand. In fact, the studio's two key directors are so acerbic in their commentary that a more cynical reading of the Ghibli filmography might lead us to the conclusion that the problem, in a nutshell, is *us*.

A conclusion which – sadly – isn't entirely without merit.

Take *Ponyo on the Cliff by the Sea*: ostensibly a film that is – if not for – geared more toward children than other Ghibli releases. Beyond that, what we have in *Ponyo* is a timely fable about, and stick with me here, a fish with a weird wizard for a father and an enormous ocean goddess for a mother, who effectively brings about a new age for the Earth – and an end to the Anthropocene.

It is a film of mixed messages. The new world is, in some ways, clearly better than the old: nature is thriving, species thought once to be extinct have returned to swim in rivers that – just days before – were bustling roads. Even people, for the most part, seem happy enough to be paddling about on their boats and enjoying a sense of new-found serenity. Or, the ones who survived the accidental cataclysm caused by Ponyo's arrival on land, at least. There is also much talk about the less apparent virtues of humanity – where Liam Neeson's Fujimoto, an ex-human himself and father to Ponyo, seems adamant that humankind ought not be given a second chance to mess things up (as surely, inevitably, they will), Ponyo and Sōsuke, her human paramour, along with both children's mothers, are determined to find a less apocalyptical (read: genocidal) solution.

As you can probably tell, and as you'll very well know if you've seen the film, the plot of *Ponyo* is somewhat convoluted even in its simplicity, following the titular character – whose given name is actually Brunhilde (which feels like a nod to the kind of folklore which *Ponyo* owes a heavy debt) – in her journey from fish, to half-fish, to quasi-human, and the connections which she makes along the way; in particular, the quickly established love between Ponyo and Sōsuke – which, though it's unclear, seems to be purely platonic. All of which runs parallel to the aforementioned oceanic Armageddon.

It is a film that hurts in strange ways, both a joyful and painful watch. It is impossible to sit through *Ponyo* as a work of fantasy without also being confronted with a stark reality – to rejoice in the reclamation of the natural world from the blight of humankind without the pang of knowing that you, despite of what may well be your best efforts, are a part of that blight.

That the planet might just be better off without you is a lot to take in – especially for kids, but, then again, if Miyazaki's point is that adulthood finds us jaded and disenfranchised, then it's the young who most need reaching with stories like *Ponyo*; those not yet ingrained with those concrete facts of life we spoke about before. If this holds true, it's an admirable goal which makes the eventual simplification down to the familiar theme of Love Conquers All a little easier to stomach here: if the choice is love, and capital-L "Love" in the grander sense, versus death – annihilation, even – then the choice itself surely becomes more obvious. Yes, it's a little close to the Fear-Love scale from *Donnie Darko*, but – presented with the choice – I know which I'd chose.

Ponyo, more than many others, is a joyful affair for the most part: in its "final test" set-piece, it gives us the chance to consider what we might lose before that loss is imposed upon us. It alludes to grief – impending, possible, but by no means certain, and is, among other things, a nod to Miyazaki's more hopeful side and a rare proof that he still thinks a better world is possible.

Only, of course, if things change.

Other stories in the Ghibli filmography are not quite as soft at the edges or as easy a pill to swallow. It's a kind of cheat to mention *Nausicaä of the Valley of the Wind*, given that it isn't *technically* a Ghibli film, but it certainly falls in line with its ethos, or set the tone for what would *become* the studio's ethos.

In *Nausicaä*, there is no choice. We open in a world already ravaged by pollution – a toxified planet, not so much dying as on the brink of death, drained of life at the hands of war and industry. We open to a population which is already grieving: grieving the continued death of friends, of family, of society – and the death, now one-thousand years ago, of the world itself. It is a hard watch – not in the way that *Grave of the Fireflies* is a hard watch, with its realism and its intimacy, but in the sense that speculative fiction so often makes for difficult viewing: yes, it is the future, whatever has happened may not have happened yet, but the clear implication is that it could – and that, if things go unchanged, it will.

A prophecy, a saviour, the chance for a new beginning with a new way of thinking. These are the hallmarks of Miyazaki-esque environmentalism: not just in *Nausicaä*, but also in films like *Laputa: Castle in the Sky*, and like *Ponyo*. And – of course – in *Princess Mononoke*; an epic battle between ancient forest gods, money-hungry con artists, greedy industrialists, and the worst and better parts of human nature.

In *Mononoke*, pre-industrial civilisation is on the brink of collapse – the old gods are dying and the new gods have human faces, deriving their power from influence and from money. From ownership over a world which, previously, had no master but itself. In the titular character – nature has its own protector: a human who exists outside of the human world, in harmony with the deep magic of the world itself.

What is most curious about this, about Mononoke herself – beyond the fact she was raised by wolf gods, wears a yokai mask, and has no particular qualms about the killing of what, on a base level, would be considered her fellow man – is that Miyazaki chose to include her in this story at all. Now, this might seem odd: she's the title character, after all. Her very existence alludes to something which crops up again and again: the fact that, while nature is armed with some mechanisms by which to defend itself – some useful remedies to use in ridding itself of the human parasite that saps its vitality more and more each day – it cannot do so alone. To affect the kind of change which might possibly make a difference to our shared future requires intervention – a cessation of hostilities toward the planet, we appear to be told, is not enough, certainly not if we wish to share in whatever the next stage of this world might look like.

Instead, Mononoke tells us, we are required to look both forward and backward – not toward ruin, but toward possibility. We are required to fight. To grieve is not enough – and to grieve, in this instance, to accept that loss, is to grieve in totality: a darkness from which there is no possible return. What this means in practice, as with all griefs of all kinds, is first to find some acceptance: not to accept that the situation is beyond us, but to accept that it is – whether we like it or not – happening to us and because of us. It is a wrong that cannot be left to right itself and which burying our heads in the sand cannot redress any more than it can undo the death of a loved one or the suppression of our spirit.

What Mononoke tells us, too, in the same way that *My Neighbor Totoro* does, is that things might get worse – in fact, they probably will, but that embracing this is not the same as giving up; the opposite, in fact. Allowing the possibility – the probability, even – of a future, both near and distant, that is worse than the one we live in now, is the key to moving forward in a different direction. Knowing that there is always room for things to get worse and to deteriorate further – whether those things be personal or societal or global in nature – is the kind of shock to the system which pushes us toward re-thinking the meaning of inevitability.

If we are accepting this is indeed a shock to the system, it feels counterintuitive, counterproductive, perhaps even counter-human, to be so cavalier in defeatism, but this is a misreading. It is not defeat – it is loss, grief. It is understanding and processing what is gone, what must be mourned and buried or burned, in order to more clearly see what might be saved and to find room in our lives for a future that is different now to the one we were promised.

We may not be able to prevent all disasters – we cannot stop the people we love from dying and though there is damage already done to this planet which we cannot now reverse, we can mitigate them. For ourselves, in our own lives, and for ourselves in the lives which will hopefully follow ours under slightly better circumstances

– and who will, if not shielded from the truth, if not fed untruths about the nature of life, know a better way from the off.

It is both difficult and painful. It is, to put it mildly, a pit of guilt and despair knowing what we have been party to, colluded in, or even just allowed to happen through pitiful inaction. What we must accept – in the face of insurmountable evidence – is the reality of loss on a scale hard to comprehend.

If you do not see the danger, then you're not going to move out of its way, are you?

*

As well as an instruction manual, these films are a love letter. True, they are addressed to a lover who has been deeply spurned and who may never quite forgive us, but they show a love that is real – one which is honest and, in many senses, vital.

The ways in which nature is rendered – the vivid colours of the sunsets and the clouds which opened this book – are the last-ditch efforts, the works of someone who so clearly cares deeply and intimately, to show us not just what the world could look like without us, but also to show the world how, in our heart of hearts, we perceive it; how much it means to us – not just as a thing of sustenance, but as a thing of beauty and of wonder. A thing of awe.

In a way, it doesn't really matter if the world – in whatever form that takes – ever receives that letter. It is the act of writing which is the act of love. It is these acts and declarations of love – even as our satellites show the world turning, all too quickly, into ash and dust before our eyes – which Studio Ghibli offers us as a way to turn things around: a bright, utopian vision which both forces us to reckon with what can no longer be and shows us that a different way is possible if we are willing to take those losses now.

Chapter 5

Grief is a myth,
and myths are real

"We tell ourselves stories in order to live," says Joan Didion in the title essay of her 1979 collection, *The White Album*. As is almost always the case with Didion, it's an affecting piece of work – concise, empathetic, shrewd and cutting. Perhaps no part more so than that quietly devastating introduction: a pronouncement that cleaves to the core not only her own writing and her own well-documented experiences with grief and loss, but also of something more universal. Something more ancient and, perhaps, something more human.

Stories, after all, are all myths of a sort. Or at least the good ones are, anyway. Yes: they are cultural artifacts with intrinsic value of their own, but they are also frameworks of a kind – lenses, handed to us as a way of viewing, interpreting, and hopefully understanding a chaotic, often cruel-seeming world.

One of the most interesting things about myths, at least in my opinion, is that they exist on a kind of pre-built yet perpetually rearrangeable scaffold system – a Lego set with which you are free to create, often with what feels like wild abandon, but in reality only within the remit of what the blocks allow.

Studio Ghibli's *Ponyo on the Cliff by the Sea* – the story of a fish who turns into a girl, submerging herself in the trappings and freedoms of the human world – has a lot in common with Hans Christian Anderson's *The Little Mermaid*, a story which, in turn, has an awful lot in common with the Greek myth of Orpheus and Eurydice.

It's not alone: *Howl's Moving Castle* and *Laputa* are loose reimaginings of the myth of Prometheus – about the trials and tribulations of stealing fire from the gods, not to share with mankind at large, but for selfish reasons. Porco Rosso, much like the doomed airship in *Kiki's Delivery Service*, flies too close to the sun. *Mononoke*'s Ashitaka has more than a hint of Theseus about him – the legendary Greek hero being not only an exile, but also tasked with the slaying of the Minotaur. And Chihiro, among other things, lured into the spirit world against her will, is a kind of avatar for

Persephone – *Spirited Away* a mirror for her abduction into the underworld.

I say this to highlight a common thread. To say that, with what they have to teach us and how they impart that wisdom, what is also interesting is that these ready-made structures are inherently practical. That they are useful in their fictions – pointing not toward the facts of life and death, living and dying, themselves but instead toward a way of understanding them. That, perhaps in spite of – or perhaps even because of – their fantastical element, they are also permutations of the truth. Or, at least, a truth: an old truth, an inescapable truth.

*

Perhaps because we are taught them at school, from a young age – although often with their integral and essential brutality either dulled or entirely removed – there is a tendency to think of mythologies as "basic" or rudimentary storytelling; to shrug them off as childish narratives, created to placate a "less developed" culture from whose naivety we are now evolved enough to set ourselves apart.

We know, after all, with the benefit of our present-day wisdom, that the sun is not dragged across the sky in the gleaming chariot of the god Apollo (or on the barge of Ra, or the carriage of Sól) – rather that its graceful rise and fall, affecting every aspect of life on this planet, is dictated by a complex and immutable set of stellar physics; we are at the whim, not of known deities with our best interests in mind as their loyal subjects, but of mathematical principles which act with no element of care or benevolence, incapable of appeasement or empathy, but functioning simply because it is the way of things.

Now, I don't know about you, but I'm not sure I prefer that way of thinking at all. There are the facts of life – and there are also, parallel to that, the facts of death. There are the rules by which we are bound and the forces at work which, for the most part invisible to the naked eye, dictate our every move. I am willing to believe, at least, that there there is more: not anything that would make sense of the ultimate chaos of being and ceasing to be, exactly, but something deeper.

Not meaning, even. Just – well – *more*.

To every myth, then – no matter how at odds with our ideas about what we know as enlightened citizens of the twenty-first century; or what we think we know, anyhow – there is a kernel of truth.

Sure, maybe there's no one up there pulling the sun across the sky – whatever. But there is a sunrise and a sunset regardless. Is it such a bad thing to give that – to give any of it, really – some sense of gravity? Not to say that the daily journey of our solar system's biggest star across the sky means any more than the physics of it all, but that it can mean more to us – that we can understand it in terms beyond those surface facts. Not the much and rightly maligned "alternative facts" that have so come to define our age, but something more like parallel truths.

There may well be no "answers" – no response to the great big *Why* of it all – but that doesn't mean that questioning it all, fleshing out the bare bones with stories of our own, can't make the fabric of life and death a richer, more vivid colour. Like Joan says: we tell ourselves stories in order to live – or, more accurately, to make life worth living.

Of course, Miyazaki and Takahata know this. More than that – they understand this.

As directors – as artists – they have, either through choice or necessity, or some combination of both, made a decision to live this way: to tell these stories. Both men have seen, lived through, and endured things that most of us could scarcely imagine for their cruelty and their chaos. Takahata's *Grave of the Fireflies* is testament to this: as clear-cut an example as there ever could be of what the anthropologist Mary Midgley called "the myths we live by" in her book of the same name.

Midgley's work, rather than an exercise in luddism or childish wish fulfilment, makes the case for mythologies as a core part of the nature and reality of being:

something like an instruction manual and in matters of reality and spirituality – the head and the heart. They are – like grief itself, in all its brutal reality and its escapism – a way of living and of, perhaps most importantly, coping with living and its flip side.

In *Grave of the Fireflies*, Seita and Setsuko – faced with the horrors of death and destruction, both at-large and far too close to home – have no choice but to begin a process of mythologising; of weaving a parallel narrative to their stark and dreadful reality. In some ways, that life is a fantasy: the siblings are orphaned, their home destroyed, and Setsuko is dying, but in others it is no less real – no less evidenced in the world around them – than the dire facts of their situation. This parallel thread, gossamer thin but which they nonetheless clutch with such white-knuckle determination, is not a hinderance to accepting their predicament but their only chance to survive it. Their only way to just keep going, when going on seems impossible. Something we all need – more often than we care to admit, perhaps.

The stakes may seem lower, but the same is true of Chihiro in *Spirited Away*: that there exists a parallel world, suddenly accessible to her only at the point her world as she knows it is completely upended, and through which she is able to better get a handle on her "real life", is a kind of mythological lens pointed at her transition from childhood to her role as young adult. This is not to say that the events of *Spirited Away* are fantasy – that it was all a dream – which would be lazy and extremely un-Miyazaki; myths, even those which may seem quaint as an impartial observer, are always real from the inside. Tangible in the moment.

At least, as much as anything else.

*

When we think of myths, we may think of these frameworks – these structures and templates; the ways in which they explained the inexplicable before we had other means to do so. We may think of how they transpose onto modern stories – how those well-trodden Greek mythologies make their way into the works of Studio Ghibli, amongst others, following their format with modern bells and whistles, but there is more to it than that. More to Ghibli's mythological entanglement. These unique modern myths are stories not of tragedy, in the traditional sense, but of grief, in a very real, very close, and very contemporary way.

These are stories of loss, played out through fantasy, to show us the truth: to show us what we need to see: when, coming in plainer terms, we might flinch and look away, these films – in all their beauty and their humour and their artistry – ask us to keep looking. To fix our eyes on the uncomfortable truth; to accept what is most difficult to accept, giving us a way to process that chaos and that pain.

Grief, after all, is the biggest myth of all: not in the sense that it is a falsehood – sadly it is not – but in the sense that it is necessary; as a way to work through the brutality of loss, and in the sense that it runs parallel to life as we know it. One does not stop happening while the other takes hold – they are entangled, for better and for worse.

Like Seita and Setsuko, like Chihiro – like Sophie Hatter who disappears from her dreary life into a world of talking fireballs and melting wizards – the myth of grief is not just a case of falling down the rabbit hole to escape reality. It's about what happens to us on the descent, what happens once we're down there, and in which ways we are profoundly changed forever once we re-emerge – if, that is, we're lucky enough to do so.

It is a different kind of myth: one which doesn't so much offer up the answers as it does provide a way to find them for ourselves. It is a maze – a labyrinth – in which we are sent to become lost before the possibility of escape is even contemplated. It is not quick – it is not easy. There is no map, no key, no legend and no scale. There is only the maze itself and the quiet echoes of the world above.

A shelter until the moment it becomes a prison, grief is the myth we live by when living feels impossible.

Yes, we tell ourselves stories in order to live. We also tell them in order to grieve. In order to lose. In order to live again. To live *still*.

Epilogue

"Life is suffering. It is hard. The world is cursed. But still, you find reasons to keep on living." – *Princess Mononoke*

When I began writing this book, I did so with some distance from grief. Or, at least, with the self-assuredness that the illusion of distance from grief can bring. At the start of 2022, I was four years on from my most recent major familial loss – the death of my grandmother – in mid-2018, some fifteen years after the passing of her husband.

This was a comfortable place to be. My life in general was – and very much still is – a considerably better place to live now, even than it was four years ago. I have a nice home by the sea, which I rent with the person I love most of all – and who, by the time this book is in your hands, I will have married.

But comfort, as is far too often the case, allows for complacency. It becomes too easy, preferable even, to begin believing – convincing yourself more with every passing day that is marked, more than anything, by its proximity to joy and to love – that there are no more bad things left to happen. The truth, though, is that we can see much less far into the future than we think – that the horizon isn't the end point, but only the illusory end point of our very limited vision.

So, inevitably, bad things will – and do – happen. Inevitably too, you are never ready when they do, because that storm is always somewhere just over the skyline until the moment that it isn't – only visible when it's far too late to hunker down. Revealing itself at first in the form of a light mist – a drizzle far too easy to ignore – before the screeching winds and emphatic claps of thunder, impossible to hear from a distance, are all of a sudden all around.

This is where I found myself, somewhere toward the middle of writing this book, when grief once again disturbed the clear and calm waters of life. Looking at what I'd written and realising that, in the context of new grief and new loss – which is such good friends with old grief, bringing that long-lost acquaintance to the party with no thought to invitation, ready to pick up just where it left off – the words were blurry, sodden, and falling to useless tatters every time I tried to read them.

I will not talk too much about this loss. It is still too fresh as I write this. It is also not entirely mine to share. It is a shared loss, which in some sense is a lighter burden to bear and in others, somehow, is a much heavier yolk. I will say that I am older now than I was then – when over twenty years ago now I allowed myself to bury grief and for it, in turn, to bury me.

As I write, I am thirty-two years old and, for my own benefit and the sake of those I love the most, I have not hidden from this loss. In part, because I have not been able to, but also because I now know better. I know, two decades on from that first cataclysmic loss, and pushing towards half a decade since the last, that you can never be ready – or, at least, that you can never be ready enough; but I also know that knowing what is coming, accepting that the ground is about to shift beneath your feet, is the only way to stay even close to steady. I am not saying that I have kept a sure footing for every moment of these last few months: we all stumble, we all trip, we all fall from time to time, but in those moments, which I will not lie and say have been infrequent, I have gone against my instincts and opted not to fight the vertigo; I have chosen, instead, to let myself go. To roll with the punches and save my energy for the kinds of battles you can win.

Perhaps, not for battles at all. As it turns out, what can take the most from you is the act of not struggling against the inevitable current in the first place. The act

– which goes against every fibre of your being and every desperate desire to act as if nothing is wrong and nothing has changed – of not acting when it feels as though circumstances demand it most. The embrace of total surrender.

You will know, I hope, if you have made it here, that sometimes the only way to gain some semblance of control is to relinquish it – to feel every wave, let them each pass through you as you pass through them in turn, allowing the salt get in your eyes and in your ears and asking the rushing darkness to envelop you – rather than pretending for a single second that you can jump above their peaks for any real amount of time. Because you can't. Don't try. It is tiring. It is useless. It is no way to live.

That's exactly what you have to do. After all, there is always – somewhere out there – a winking light in the darkness.

References

Chapter 1

1. "The Animated Life." Daniel Cappello, *The New Yorker*, 9 January 2005. newyorker.com/magazine/2005/01/17/the-animated-life. Accessed 11 October 2022.
2. "Isao Takahata's stark world of reality." Masami Ito, *The Japan Times*, 12 September 2015. japantimes.co.jp/culture/2015/09/12/films/isao-takahatas-stark-world-reality/. Accessed 11 October 2022.

Chapter 2

1. ""Why Must Fireflies Die So Young?": Isao Takahata's Masterpiece 30 Years On." Karl Smith, *The Quietus*, 13 April 2018. thequietus.com/articles/24387-isao-takahata-grave-of-the-fireflies. Accessed 11 October 2022.
2. Ibid.

Chapter 3

1. "Every Studio Ghibli Film Is Secretly About The Same Thing." William Kuechenberg, *Cracked*, 23 February 2022. cracked.com/article_32751_every-studio-ghibli-film-is-secretly-about-the-same-thing.html. Accessed 11 October 2022.

Acknowledgements

With eternal thanks to Marianne Eloise – whom over the course of writing this book became my wife and who, over the last few years and since the moment that we met, has shown me what it means to be alive. And, of course, what it means to be loved.

To my parents, for their continued support and for letting my live in their house for far too long.

To Mia; a sister-in-law and a sister in every other sense of the word.

To Heather and to Laura at 404: thank you for your guidance and, above all else, your patience which I have so thoroughly tested.

To Morris and Mary Page, and to Norman Atkins. Forever winking lights in the darkness.

About the author

Karl Thomas Smith is a writer covering fashion, music, film, and other arts-adjacent topics across the broad culture spectrum for outlets including *Dazed*, *Highsnobiety*, *i-D*, etc. Previously an editor at *HYPEBEAST* and *The Quietus*, he lives in Brighton with his wife, Marianne, and their dog, Bowie. He can usually be found cooking. @karlthomassmith

About the Inklings series

This book is part of 404 Ink's Inkling series which presents big ideas in pocket-sized books.

They are all available at 404ink.com/shop.

If you enjoyed this book, you may also enjoy these titles in the series:

The Loki Variations – Karl Johnson

By exploring contemporary variations of Loki, from Norse god to anti-hero trickster, we can better understand the power of myth, queer theory, fandom, ritual, pop culture itself and more.

Love That Journey For Me – Emily Garside

Considering the fusion of existing sitcom traditions, references and tropes, this Inkling analyses the nuance of *Schitt's Creek* and its surrounding cultural and societal impact as a queer revolution.